When the Ice Melts

poems by

Laura Glenn

Finishing Line Press
Georgetown, Kentucky

When the Ice Melts

Copyright © 2016 by Laura Glenn
ISBN 978-1-63534-079-2 First Edition
All rights reserved under International and Pan-American Copyright Conventions.
No part of this book may be reproduced in any manner whatsoever without written permission from the publisher, except in the case of brief quotations embodied in critical articles and reviews.

ACKNOWLEDGMENTS

Some of the poems in this book first appeared in other publications, occasionally with slight variations. A grateful acknowledgment is made to the editors.

"After Feeding Your Cat" appeared in *Voices from the Porch*.
"Between a Rock and a Soft Space" appeared in *Indian River Review*.
"Brick Wall" and "Retreat" appeared in *Brick Plight*.
"Cybermom" appeared in *Steam Ticket*.
"Depth Perception" and "Shred" appeared in *Healing Muse;* "Depth Perception" also
    appeared in *From the Finger Lakes: A Poetry Anthology*.
"Eggshells" appeared in *Constellations*.
"Eternity" and "Ten Boxes of Poems Reduced to One" appeared in *Blast Furnace*.
"Flight" appeared in *Green Mountains Review*.
"The Log-Book" appeared in *The Cortland Review*.
"Planktonic" appeared in *Common Ground*.
"Skating" appeared in *Buffalo Bones*.
"Slickwater" appeared in *Vigil for the Marcellus Shale*.
"Venice Unshuttered" appeared in *StepAway Magazine*.

Thanks go to AE Ventures for a grant for my exuberant and productive retreat in Montreal. I also thank CAP for a Specific Opportunity Stipend for a much-needed calm mini-retreat to the Saltonstall Foundation to complete work on this chapbook.

Special thanks for encouragement and help along the way also go to Paul Cody and Liz Holmes, Pat Duffy, Susan and Stephen Hesse, Alice Fulton, Emily Rhoads Johnson, Catharine O'Neill, Dan Otis, Ellen Peckham, Camille Roman, and David Weiss, among others. For continued critiques and conviviality, I am grateful to members of my poetry group, Cory Brown, Peter Fortunato, Gail Holst-Warhaft, and Jack Hopper. For being there, I also thank Nick and the rest of my family.

Publisher: Leah Maines
Editor: Christen Kincaid
Cover Art: Laura Glenn, *Ascending*
Author Photo: Laura Glenn
Cover Design: Elizabeth Maines

Printed in the USA on acid-free paper.
Order online: www.finishinglinepress.com
    also available on amazon.com

Author inquiries and mail orders:
Finishing Line Press
P.O. Box 1626
Georgetown, Kentucky 40324
U.S.A.

Table of Contents

Eggshells 1

Shred 3

Depth Perception 4

Eternity 6

Log-Book 7

The Princess and the Pea 8

Juggled 9

Brick Wall 10

Writer's Retreat 12

Cybermom 14

Skating 16

Ice Creek 17

Slickwater 19

Planktonic 20

Retreat: Monet's Haystacks 21

Flight 22

February Fourteenth 23

Ten Boxes of Poems Reduced to One 25

Venice Unshuttered 26

Between a Rock and a Soft Space 28

After Feeding Your Cat 30

Eggshells

When I hear the expression
like walking on eggshells
I picture trampling them to a dry mosaic.

If they're already broken and empty,
who cares if I walk on them?
And if they're whole,
the image seems too absurd.

Perhaps there's reason to tiptoe back
across the eggshell-strewn room—
trying to walk so lightly

as not to break more,
while the pieces crumble,
smaller and smaller—

and the one
I must be careful with
sits there,
ignoring the delicate crunch.

When I hear the expression,
it's not apt
but I imagine the pleasure
of crushing eggshells—

the curves giving way to flatness—
then looking down
at the crazing pattern
underfoot. For one long moment

this image distracts me
from pondering
my fear of abandonment,

and having to be so careful,
when no matter what I do or say
it seems I can't elude damage.

Then a memory of dread
descends—a memory of

feeling broken to smithereens.

Shred

Dad hands me a confidential paper.
Together we turn bipolar
disorders into a snow of confetti: it blows
onto the garden of rug.

We switch blades: I destroy suicidal impulses—cut
self-destructive tendencies to ribbons, blithely make fortunes
you could tuck into cookies from obsessions and compulsions,
crank spaghetti out of eating disorders, toss word salads in the garbage;

our progress slowed by his cloudy eyes
lingering on each page before he hands it to me to destroy, blindly.
My father has always been excellent
about confidentiality;

I never quite grasped what he did for a living
until I was sent to one.
So actually I have no idea
what we're shredding: all the forbidden subjects.

I could snatch a few strands—stuff them in my pocket,
later, paste them together, randomly, like a dadaist poet.
Maybe he knows what I'm thinking:
above the clamor he jokes that he could shred me.

I tell my dada, who loves puns, "I could be a cutup."
Then it's back to business: I want him to know he can trust me.
I shred another paper, helping
my parents clear out the old house

they're too old to manage.
While I'm with my father in his office,
tearing life stories to shreds,
my mother's in the bedroom shedding reams of tears.

Depth Perception

Last year,
walking this path,
wind blew through a pine tree—
for an instant I saw the ghost of the tree
made entirely of pollen, and shaped like a pine,
float through the air.

Something about this evening light:
distant streetlights cast long reflections
across the lake—shrouded, amber-tinted,
and shaped like upright bodies
bandaged by the light
like mummies,
though I also think: Ganges.

"It's the dead," I say
and start to cry.
"Father," I whisper.
I start to connect
to one of the reflections
—they're like cocoons—
as if something might emerge,
and my father and I might continue
things said and left unsaid,
heard and not heard.

Down the lake
of time, the reflections appear
in sequence—staggered—and stagnant
for the moment, like the gone.

My father loved travel—
India, Egypt, everywhere.
Where are you going now,
brave voyager?

As solid looking as the lamp lights' reflections,
reflections of car lights
move fast,
as if there's no one here
they need to stop and see.

I head home on my walk,
treading soft needles to humus.
My father, with his gift
for making something
of life, now is light on water: illumined;

swaddled, like a mummy,
about to start a new life . . .
and some part of me can't stop entertaining
thoughts I don't believe in.

Eternity

> *For what are Stars but Asterisks*
> *To point a human Life?**

In the dark planetarium
of your imagination,
you wonder,
if Dickinson were alive today,
how bold would she be,
how public, like a blog?

See that constellation
connected in cyberspace?
Not Virgo, with her shaft of wheat,
but Emily Dickinson
—pen in hand—
in her long white dress.

Among the stars, countless
as the number of times Emily
considered "Eternity"—
imagine her bending rules
on the Internet, or self-promoting,
then keening, exulting.

From that domed, pensive place—
think of Dickinson wheeling
through cyberspace: If she stumbled,
or if she were dissed,
would her diadem of stars

scatter like wildflowers
on a field of study—
or shatter to dust of nebula?

*E.D.

The Log-Book

Climbing the swayback hill
by Bird Cemetery Road,
my feet sink into mud,
the small bones—roots.

I'm turning into a bush
of burrs that want me
to carry their seeds.
Picking the little porcupines off

I stump into a log—
it splinters into pages—
detailed with worms.
Abandoning that log-book,

I stagger up
toward a tree
with a blue hole: blue center.
I want to forget those worms.

The tree, firmly rooted,
arches beyond the ledge
overlooking the patchwork comforter
of fields. Approaching

the windswept tree,
my shadow flings
itself over—flies a little
and returns.

The Princess and the Pea

Books stack up like mattresses
in "The Princess and the Pea."

I reach for the tome I'm reading—
heavy as a tomb and just as grave

as the grimmest fairy tale—
but dreading the downward spiral

toward nightmares or insomnia,
end up grabbing a pencil,

finding a part of a page
where I haven't planted rows of words . . .

I jot down something ordinary,
say, *worthwhile*, *accomplishment*, even *lullaby*;

nothing negative, *desperation*, *betrayal*;
or tiresome like *potential*,

then prod as many words as I can from its letters: so many peas
tumble from each pod,

left empty, a minute boat
that could drift off—moored by a curlicue of heed.

Wanting sleep, I shell word after word—anything
to stop the circling train of thought—

until one last word,
gentle as a pea-green pill,

dissolves:

Juggled

Just when I find that still space
in the center,
you can hear a pin crash!

Lately, I've been feeling like pins
whirling through the air.
Up we go again.

Who's the juggler?
Why are sparklers added?

A shower of fiery angels
spark from heads of pins,
circle like fireworks

in daylight.
More pins drop.

Douse the burning grass
in a shower of water.
Please, do not add knives . . .

So many selves flying flaming
—faster, faster—
spinning till they disappear,

as if I didn't know
what's coming:
extinguish me anew.

Sometimes a force almost
beyond me helps to pick me
up in the air again;

sometimes, for a long moment,
everything stays there.

Brick Wall

A little group, roughly my age,
relaxes in lounge chairs outside
a brick building.
I sense the easy connection
between them ≈ warm waves in cool air.
They don't look familiar,
yet I recognize them
as people I half-know.
Without saying, I make it clear I want
to share the intimacy.

So, I'm delighted to be handed
an orange brick—
feel its rough heft,
and see my initials baked in;
until now I hadn't noticed
the small letters
scattered across the wall—
or the brick-shaped opening
lined with mortar.

I insert the brick—viscous paste
blurring the lines
around the edges—and complete
the staggered pattern.

When I try to align
the brick, I lean against the wall;
it gives way—
like a revolving door
I stagger through.

On the other side,
I'm alone now
in a room with an exposed
brick wall,
a tidy bed with comforter
of delicate flowers and vines,
a desk and chair,

and these words—each
a brick of varying size.

I start to build
the end, or beginning,
of the dream.

Writer's Retreat

Breezing through the city,
weaving in and out of galleries,
watching light bounce patterns off windows
full of flouncy clothes—I fear
I'm just a *flaneur*. I enter a café—
treat myself to latte, pull out the Montblanc
I was gifted years ago: I'm no mountebank.
The authentic self is where? It's good
to explain I'm in Montreal
writing, exploring, renewing,
while I ground myself
visiting my son: when I feel unreal
this validates me: "No one can be a poet
all the time," a teacher once said; constantly creating
even myself—a work in progress, in motion, commotion,
not accomplishing

enough: I hole myself up
in a room with an exposed
brick wall—a castlet, mini-monastery.
Or am I confusing *gaol* and *goal*?
There's a block-wide power outage.
Time stops: the clock doesn't blink.
There's a candle holder, but no candle;
an oil lamp, but no oil.
I'm in the ink-to-paper stage,
working by the light of my computer.
If blocked I'm undeserving. Who can think
and feel deeply, perceive uniquely
all the time? My pen runs out;
I etch the page sans ink—
my best lines invisible.

For company I read mail: On short notice
I'm invited to a literary costume party.
Away from home, can I pull this off?
I could go as myself: too arrogant.
I fret in the dark, then dream of masked identities.
Come daylight I'm squandering time
in the tacky Halloween store: a mustache speaks to me.
I stop at the local *epicerie* for a bag of madeleines;
then don black pants and jacket I hide
my braid in. I stick on the 'stache,
and scalloped sweets in hand,
who wouldn't know I'm Proust?
But the room I enter is full of plainclothes writers;
one even says, "I came as myself."
So I take the prize
and in my meager French say,
"*Je m'appelle Marcel.*"

Cybermom

I talk to you on the screen.
So what if I can't kiss your forehead,
smell your hair? Hair long, hair short, beard on, beard off;
I watch you play with time playing with you.
Sometimes you pixellate
like a Chuck Close painting: Still, I feel close to you.

And grateful for Skype: How else
would I make it through
months going on years away from you?
Or, maybe it's gotten too easy
to feel connected, maybe
if not for Skype we'd see each other more.

Your father and I watch DVDs on the large TV
you bought back in high school
with money earned on eBay;
otherwise we haven't touched
a thing in your room.

Except the fish tank that livened your desk.
In early autumn, I hauled the glass box
to the duckweed pond
and released tiny frogs
I grew from tadpoles. All that's left
is a snail named Ed Sullivan.

As a young child, I imagined tiny people
inhabiting the TV—like fish in a tank.
Now you're my favorite show.
I watch you and you watch me, or
we glimpse ourselves on small squares
beneath the larger ones.

You can turn me off
when I start to dispense
advice like an annoying ad.
Or you can e-mail me something we're talking about
while Skyping; I can shoot you this poem—
read it across cyberspace.

It's always a treat to see you.
It's not half bad
to be half-robot,
though sometimes I'm half-sad.

Skating

I haven't done it
in ages, since high school,
when I wasn't afraid to fall.

This fall
I take my son to the rink,
not steady enough to take his hand.

He recklessly races ice circles around me.
Stiff-legged—I totter on blades—
balanced by thoughts
of cracked teeth, broken bones, and age.

My once "double-jointed" legs loosen
when John Lennon returns from the dead
to rhythmically urge me
back to the past.

My blades kick up a ghostly dust
of sparks and mist.

Around and around I skate,
farther and farther from the safety edge—
a needle circling the groove of an old record.

After a near-trip I stop to loosen
the laces around my achy ankles.
My rosy-cheeked boy flies by.

Still for a long moment, frozen in a track
in my brain, a meaningless word repeatedly repeated
on a scratched record: *Fear*

holds me back,
plays and plays.

Ice Creek

The green engineer says, knowledge
ruins his appreciation
of beauty. Even sunsets—
shell-pink blurring into lavender,
a nacreous cloud, glorious with pollution.

Weren't there sunsets
before? Even if sometimes
it makes the sky beautiful,
must I despise the colors?
I worry about warming;
but still, the colors!

Maybe I don't feel bad enough.
Today, the creek overflows.
Water rises; sump pumps
do overtime, as do firefighters—
bailing out basements.

City workers barge in, smash
ice chunks that jam the creek—
claw them out with the long arm
and huge hand of a scoop crane.
Leafless lilacs along the creek
lose limbs.

Crushes of ice in bitter water rush
under the bridge
lined with watchful neighbors.
Kids pause by roads turned
into barricaded ice rinks.

Toward evening, volunteers pass sandbags—
pile them like plump pillows
to ward off watery nightmares,
fitful sleep. The unfrozen waterfall
roars in the background.

I find a beautiful thing in the mess:
a rain-darkened lilac branch
sprinkled with celadon-green lichen—it twists
and ramifies, narrows at zigzag angles,
bears delicate blooms of fungus,
like cherry blossoms.

Maybe the young engineer was right.
Ice creaks like an old door opening.
Crossing a bridge, absorbed
in the branch I brandish home,
a layer of feelings begins to thaw and mix.

I sidestep a puddle hosting an oily rainbow.

Slickwater

X marks the spot, you're told
you're sitting on gold.
Dirt poor and famished
and now they place a plate of salad greens
before you: picked from the field—
not a wilted or brown-edged leaf on top—
and fragrantly seasoned, piquant.

You pick up your fork, ready
to lift the first mouthful
of glistening lettuce to your lips.
Midair the leaves look like money—
fresh bills: too many
to consume in one sitting.

But this is no green money.
For what is in the oil the salad
is lightly dressed in?
And how to wash this down?

Down the road
when your well's ruined,
armed men will bring you fresh water
by the truckload—provided
you sign the nondisclosure form by the X.

Planktonic

We drift along on the craft,
past islets of marsh grasses—green clouds of time.
The naturalist hauls up a lobster trap
entangled in seaweed—frilly, dripping brine, dotted
with jellyfish like glass gooseberries, but merrily patterned;
silver-brown fish swooped from their school; and something she
can get a grip on: snippy lobsters, pinching crabs.
She plunks them in the tank.

An osprey poses by the grass—silver bass trophy drooping from its beak.
The naturalist hoists another box: hermit crabs claw eerily from host shells.
Translucent sheets of seaweed unwrap stars,
which begin as plankton—which is anything
small that drifts on a current by the shore.
Later, the starry floaters become motile, will themselves forward.
Though weak, sea stars are tenacious—can take a week
to pry open a shellfish, get what they need. We glide along

past a thinning sandbar—like an hourglass running out of time.
Webbed feet buried in warm grains,
the silent laughing gull stares at me staring.
The heron I've been eyeing in anticipation
doesn't fly. I want to fly
onto the back of a wave
like a dolphin diving among other dolphins
into near-emerald water.

Overhead a seagull stagnates midair—
wings flapping like banners in wind—getting nowhere.
The navigator relaxes as the current brings the boat in—
leaving a wake of streamer-tentacles.
I lift my head: breathe
the good marsh air,
above the morass of green and floaty plants exhaling
so we can inhale.

Retreat: Monet's Haystacks

Monet's palette turned like a timepiece—the colors telling
the hour of day. And light revealed
when to switch the canvas, when to pack up or return to paint.

Monet's art—once outrageous, later the rage—
simulates serenity: green-aqua shadows on citrus grass,
and a touch of Rose Madder. Today my mind's alchemy

transforms Monet's grainstacks into straw huts, refuge
from the yellow sky—the sunlight that outlasts darkness.
Thatched roofs of hay protect walls of hay,

like self protecting self. The shocks
of hay betray beauty before the separation
of wheat from chaff.

Flight

I'm old fashioned: I don't
believe in adultery.
And I'd rather live
alone than like this.
I brush the crumbs
off the table
and put my shawl on to

go take a walk
for a view of air: white
sky, white clouds.
I'm sad but it doesn't matter.
I watch three crows
race to the phone wire—
one flies beyond.

Then I visit the pond
where the paranoiac gander
threatens to bite me
and geese fly off
the water as if
I could walk across it.

February Fourteenth

I'm on the street
and it's raining Magritte men,
dressed in black, dripping roses.
The roses call
attention to the men's looks
of bemused anxiety, charming
in a dazed sort of way: their eyes reflecting
clouds as they pass each other on the gray street—
their hearts outside their bodies.

One drives by with a rose
in a frill of baby's breath
propped up in the passenger seat.
Where is he going? To give
the rose in hope of a kiss
from one who is faceless, anonymous
as Magritte's cloth-swathed lovers?
Or is his heart nervous, tentative?
Is his torso an open cage with doves?

Such a contagion of roses impresses me
with sheer numbers. Later,
in the supermarket,
I watch men bearing single stems:
One man bites a plastic-sheathed stem
of rose between his teeth,
freeing his hands
to inspect eggs for cracks—or flames,
like Magritte's burning eggs.
Another man totters unsteadily—the rose,
a wineglass he holds—half empty.

I stand beside the red grapes,
and taste one to see if it's sour. Really, it's sweet
to see these men bearing single stems.
Some pause to consider blood oranges, tart
green apples—like the one superimposed
on a Magritte face.
One man shares my bafflement
at a slab of raw meat
unironically carved in a heart shape—beyond Magritte!

All the while red roses dominate, conspire collectively—
like Magritte's painting of an enormous rose,
which fills an entire room.
Compare that fragrant color on canvas
to all these scentless blooms,
as hopeful men peer at what's left
in the white bucket—roses
in shades of dried blood,
meager without being
petite, as if the bruised
and wilted outer petals
had been peeled and peeled and peeled.

Ten Boxes of Poems Reduced to One

So much for those wild years when poetry meant more
than my life and both suffered for it.
I threw away too much
for those poems; now I crumple
my paper past, vanish

evidence of colorful characters,
who haven't aged well in black and white:
vagabonds I bonded with, students
of life I studied, artists whose works drew me—
whose lives terrified.

I thought I was thinking
outside the box,
but too much ended up inside.
So I'm throwing the box away.

I read with forbearance,
then toss poems like snowballs
that managed to survive Hell—
sometimes in quadruplicate.

More than one poem I trash three times,
then spare when it resurfaces,
uncanny as a recurring dream
that garners meaning.

It gives me pause: What else in a trice
have I sloughed of my pensiveness?
Banished to the recycler,

those yellowed onionskins
become spotless, virgin white—someone else's

fresh start:

Venice Unshuttered

Long ago, I was asked if I could live
during any age
which would it be? Renaissance
sprung to mind, but I was young.
Imagine, a cloistered Renaissance woman
looking at the world through a window,
while the world viewed her,
as if in a painting, framed.

Yesterday, while taking a *vaporetto*
to a museum, I photoed
a woman, at her window
looking quaint—
unshuttered but still
planted, leaning toward sunlight.

It's morning; I fling open the shutters: see past
terra-cotta rooftops
like neatly whelmed-over plant pots,
and a windowsill planter where thyme flowers.
Laundry sways on a line;
my braid sways, too—long enough
for a ledge mouse to climb.

Beneath my third-story window
people stream across
a tiny bridge
where murmur blends with burble.
An oarsman dips and pulls
against the current—his wooden boat glides
between brick walls,
then disappears under the bridge,
ferrying today's bread.

Water divides the city the bridges connect:
to my left, a fruit stand
in front of a small bookstore;
part of the city I haven't explored yet, to my right.

If I walk farther than the eye can see,
I'll find more
water-stained buildings with pointy arched windows
~ and their watery reflections ~
some housing portraits of women,
framed by windows, their hair bejeweled—
not undone by the wind like mine has become.
I'll scoff at rabid tourism,
yet everywhere stalls of scarves
will beckon me to choose.

I look down at the stream of people, and fancy
I'm like none of them,
though soon I'm one of them, crossing
another small bridge.

Between a Rock and a Soft Space
I saw the angel in the marble and carved until I set him free.
—Michelangelo

Vague figures materialize
from cumulus clouds;
marbleize, shape-shift,
but never fully form,
like Michelangelo's unfinished
statues of slaves.

The muscular clouds writhe:
their changes
seem psychological.
They cannot break away,
even in airy softness.

Elated, in the clouds,
I think of the artist
who didn't carve enough
to free all of his figures.

Now his Unfinished Statues
are imprisoned in modernity.
One statue shoulders the rock
he's partially carved from.
Another, nearly unearthed,
seems too worn to move.

Their faces, if there at all, look effaced.
Chisel marks—hairs—appear on their legs.
Down the hall from them,
smooth David of Goliath proportions
awaits admiration.

They look older than David,
yet stuck in blocks
that some describe as wombs,
some as tombs.

Flying over the Mediterranean,
the plane passes through a cloud
like a hatchling
nosing through albumin.

I'm not afraid of flying.
I'm scared of being
worn down,
enslaved to survival.

How many times can I escape?
The clouds will regroup,
abandon the project,
dissipate, turn to rain,
rise again.

After Feeding Your Cat
—for Emily

I sit on a bench on your back porch,
overlooking the trace of green lawn
where the morning rime has melted.

Your cat, a variation on mine,
nuzzles the blunt end of my pen
while I compose
myself.

The clouds transform
both themselves and the landscape,
as they turn distant
hills into snowy mountains:
I could be far away.

Maple samaras
pinwheel down from trees in my yard
into yours.

On your side
of the separating hedge,
a crab apple tree
juts out calligraphically.

A squirrel you are wont to feed
peers at me, curls its tail
forward—an Atlas
with a huge
dandelion puff on its back,
like wishes that won't
blow away.

I don't know it
until I leave, but I stay
just long enough to gain
perspective.

Even when you're gone,
I borrow this
cup of grace.

Laura Glenn's first book of poems, *I Can't Say I'm Lost*, was published by FootHills. Her poems have appeared in many journals, including, *The Antioch Review, Boulevard, The Cortland Review, Epoch, Green Mountains Review, Literal Latté, Massachusetts Review, Poet Lore, Poetry, Rattapallax, Smartish Pace*, and the anthologies, *A Fragile Index of the World* and *From the Finger Lakes: A Poetry Anthology*. She is the recipient of a poetry grant from AE Ventures, a CAP fellowship in poetry, and a Specific Opportunity Stipend, also from CAP. A Pushcart nominee, Glenn is completing a second book-length manuscript of poems. In addition, she is working with other poets on ekphrastic projects that combine poetry and art. Also a visual artist, she lives in Ithaca, NY, where she works as a freelance editor.

www.ingramcontent.com/pod-product-compliance
Lightning Source LLC
LaVergne TN
LVHW041510070426
835507LV00012B/1460